Dear Parent:
Your child's love of reading starts here!

Every child learns to read in a different way and at his or her own speed. You can help your young reader improve and become more confident by encouraging his or her own interests and abilities. You can also guide your child's spiritual development by reading stories with biblical values and Bible stories, like I Can Read! books published by Zonderkidz. From books your child reads with you to the first books he or she reads alone, there are I Can Read! books for every stage of reading:

SHARED READING
Basic language, word repetition, and whimsical illustrations, ideal for sharing with your emergent reader.

BEGINNING READING
Short sentences, familiar words, and simple concepts for children eager to read on their own.

READING WITH HELP
Engaging stories, longer sentences, and language play for developing readers.

READING ALONE
Complex plots, challenging vocabulary, and high-interest topics for the independent reader.

ADVANCED READING
Short paragraphs, chapters, and exciting themes for the perfect bridge to chapter books.

I Can Read! books have introduced children to the joy of reading since 1957. Featuring award-winning authors and illustrators and a fabulous cast of beloved characters, I Can Read! books set the standard for beginning readers.

A lifetime of discovery begins with the magical words **"I Can Read!"**

Visit www.icanread.com for information on enriching your child's reading experience.
Visit www.zonderkidz.com for more Zonderkidz I Can Read! titles.

(Noah) sent the dove out from the ark again. In the evening the dove returned to him. There in its beak was a freshly picked olive leaf! So Noah knew that the water on the earth had gone down.

–Genesis 8:10–11

Mission City Press

Bringing Faith to Life™

The children's group
of Zondervan

www.zonderkidz.com

Noah and the Ark
Copyright © 2007 by Mission City Press. All Rights Reserved. All Beginner's Bible copyrights and trademarks (including art, text, characters, etc.) are owned by Mission City Press and licensed exclusively by Zondervan of Grand Rapids, Michigan.
ISBN-10: 0-310-71458-3
ISBN-13: 978-0-310-71458-3

Requests for information should be addressed to:
Grand Rapids, Michigan 49530

Library of Congress Cataloging-in-Publication Data

Noah and the Ark / illustrated by Kelly Pulley.
   p. cm. – (I can read)
   ISBN-13: 978-0-310-71458-3 (softcover)
   ISBN-10: 0-310-71458-3 (softcover)
   1. Noah's ark–Juvenile literature. 2. Noah (Biblical figure)–Juvenile literature. I. Pulley, Kelly, ill.
BS658.N55 2007
222'.1109505–dc22

     2006034438

Editor: Kristen Tuinstra
Art Direction: Jody Langley
Cover Design: Laura Maitner-Mason

Printed in China

07 08 09 10 11 • 10 9 8 7 6 5 4 3 2 1

The Beginner's Bible™

Noah and the Ark

Genesis 6–9

pictures by Kelly Pulley

A long time ago, people
were very mean to each other.
They forgot about God.

They did not love God.

This made God very sad.

But Noah was a good man.
Noah and his family
loved God.

God had a big plan.

He told Noah,

"I am going to start over."

God told Noah to build a boat.

The boat was called an ark.

And Noah did what God said.

God said, "I will save you.
I will save your family
and two of each animal."

Noah built the boat.

God sent the animals.

"Hi, cats and dogs!
Hi, bears and birds!"

There was food.

There was family.

There were God's animals.

One day, God closed the door.
Then God sent a big storm!

Rain began to fall.

It rained and rained.

The ark rocked and rocked.

The ark bumped up and down,
up and down.

Noah prayed.

Noah's family prayed.

The animals watched.

God took care of Noah.

God took care of his family.

God kept all of them safe.

The rain fell for days,
and days,
and days.

The earth was covered
with water!

"Shhhhh," Noah said.

Something was different.

It was quiet!

The rain had stopped!

The ark was still!

27

Noah said,

"Dove, please find land."

But Dove did not find land.

Noah said, "Dove, try again."
Dove did find land!

One day, the ark bumped
into land. Slowly, the water
started drying up.

God said, "Time to go!"

He helped Noah open the ark.

The animals went to play.

God said, "See the rainbow?
It means I will not cover the earth
with water again. I promise!"